STELLA WALKER'S ACQUAINTANCES

COLLECTED POEMS

Braeden Michaels

STELLA WALKER'S ACQUAINTANCES

COLLECTED POEMS

Braeden Michaels

Storm of Ink
2020

This is a work of poetry and prose. All characters portrayed in this book are the products of the author's imagination.

Copyright 2020 by Braeden Michaels

All rights reserved. No part of this book may be reproduced or used in any manner without express written permission from the author except in the case of quotations used in a book review in which a clear link to the source of the quote and its author is required.

First paperback edition September 2020

Front cover design by bookcoverzone.com

ISBN 978-1-7347499-2-2 (paperback)

Published by Storm of Ink
PO Box 152
Gainesville, GA USA 30503
www.braedenmichaels.com

TABLE OF CONTENTS

More Books 2

Prologue 3

Bleeding Shadows 7

Trembling Insomnia 27

Sleeping with Anxiety 43

Awakened Faith 59

Sparkling Light 77

Epilogue 96

MORE BOOKS

<u>Poetry Collection</u>
The Raven's Poison

<u>Anthologies</u>
"The Cancerous Affair"
in *Static Dreams Volume One*

Poetry in *The Poets Symphony*

PROLOGUE

Between 3:45am and 6:15am she relinquishes the lingering shadows. She lays in bed beside a voiceless ghost with tears etched on her freckles. A candle burned throughout the desolate nights. She tosses and turns within the friction. She seeks companionship without a compass. She stumbles upon acquaintances with camouflaged agendas and aggravated motives. She aches for a defined closeness. She disregards the comrades and sidekicks. Constantly questioning the sermons and religious literature.

Between 6:30am and 7:30am she clenches on to the memories like she is holding a stuffed bear. She misses the morning kisses, soft sunrise greetings, and the sound of the little ones. The word "widow" seems to be engraved on her skin. She cherished the seconds, the laughter, and the life she had as a wife. She struggles to leave her bed. She often murmurs the word nightmare under her breath. She has said a thousand prayers that feel to be not heard. She fumbles through her purse to seek her identity and sees the name "Stella Walker". She wipes away the sadness and clashes with finding a beginning.

Deep in the corner of her journey, she stumbled across a field. Blades of tall grass embraced her child-like spirit. As she glided through the wide field, her eyes lit up when came across the butterflies grazing her fingers. Some of them never left her side as she was guided through her passage. Some of the butterflies never returned. Stella trudged through the pastures with pauses, questions, and blank stares. Often, she was misguided by vagabonds, pranksters, chairmen, salesmen, artists, and a plethora of fools with invisible scars. Though at moments when she felt discouraged and misplaced, Stella continued to parade through the fields of uncertainty.

The word "widow" often glided with a stigma. Predators stood inches apart while dreamers stood six feet apart. She was often judged with disdain and apathy. Stella had a tough time keeping her chin up in the dark. She walked in the light without a compass but gravitated to the birds soaring in her fragile soul. She could feel the breeze with her sensitive heart and loneliness was like a shadow. Stella endured the cold and ached for the warmth. She watched her children tremble in grief. She observed their discontent and anxiety like a hawk.

As she sat under the crooked stars, she could hear him echo. Photographs couldn't seem to leave her mind. The snapshots and portraits only created waterfalls. All that was beautiful appeared to be so ugly. She felt like a remainder and the chaos left a carousel. Insomnia and apprehension were jittery. No one heard her screams. No one connected to her loss. No one reached for her hand with care. She was treated like a cursed diamond. Stella paraded the fields and heard the destruction from a distance.

Within the silence as she glanced at her surroundings, a seed was planted within the center of her being. A journey was ahead of her. Stella was going to embark on a path she didn't think existed. She couldn't feel or see the stages that were before her. The endings and beginnings drifted into a smog. As she walked across the bridge, she could see a faded sign above the rustic door of the aged house. As she got closer the words sent a shiver down her spine.

> *"Acquaintances will know what they want to know. Friends will want to know everything."*

BLEEDING SHADOWS

"Loneliness is a shadow until you look into the mirror."

Gwendolyn Charles

By the old-fashioned book
True conventionalist
Gripping the right wing
Ordinary and orthodox
A stand-up citizen
Common and classical
Type-A personality
Engineered by structure
Rooted and habitual
Fixed by order
Grounded for life

Colt Harrison

Overbearing and demanding

High expectations of others

Dark thin eyebrows

Relentless and a heartbreaker

A true perfectionist

Married, divorced, married, divorced

Always blaming the woman

Never looking at repetitive mistakes

Unable to look in the mirror

Sebastian Cage

Blade-like teeth sparkle

Drooling a sinister circus

Vomiting chunks of truth

After inhaling gobs of deceit

Staring at shattered mirrors

stepping into shards of identity

Cutting into a split personality

A minor loss of hearing

Slick black Dracula-like hair

Hanging his spirit like a bat

in a tortuous dying cave

As he plays a lullaby backwards

Hands quickly shrivel

Silent eyebrows howl

Character is a slow death

Stella Walker's Acquaintances

Darla Monroe

Afraid of insects
Afraid of the dark
Afraid of heights
Afraid of pain
Afraid of relationships
Afraid of death
Afraid of animals
Afraid of touch
Afraid of procreating
Afraid of living

Dorsey Cohen

A fan of Cannonball Adderley
Casual drinker of whiskey and sour
Resided in Tampa Bay, Florida
A man who loved "Carol Burnett and Friends"
Terribly shattered and lost
Married for 10 glorious years
Left him for another man
That could produce children
Now residing in Columbus, Ohio
To find the pieces of his broken heart

Claudia Jamison

Too sensitive

Too kind

Too generous

Too giving

Too sweet

Too loving

Too naive

Too used

Too hurt

Too abused

Danielle Lee

Authentically jagged

Crisp maroon edges

Revved up by the throttle

Seductively mysterious

A provocative beast

Lover of blackjack

Carrying lip-biting hunger

Tattooed and strong

Mentally rough

Hardcore in all layers

Paul Vance

"I will be back in a bit, going to get dinner from that burger place you love."
Three hours pass and she doesn't return.
The next day I come home after work and all her stuff is gone.
A month goes by and decided to text her.
"Where is my burger? I'm starving?"

Matthew Trotter

Loves stacking blocks
Loves apples and pears
Loves Bugs Bunny
Loves hiding behind the chair
Loves to snuggle
Loves to turn pages
Loves to change his mind
Loves making messes
Loves his checkered blanket
Loves his stuffed monkey
Loves to make a hearty laugh
Loves to be a toddler
Loves his mother and father

Stella Walker's Acquaintances

Debra Milton

She let out a crying whisper
She was terrified of the light
Waiting for him to answer

She ignored all the colors
She fell into the corner
Waiting for him to answer

She slept with the stranger
She hid from anyone close
Waiting for him to answer

She stared into alienation
She walked away from the signs
Waiting for him to answer

She ran from the shackles
She stood in the crossroads
Waiting for him to answer

She hobbled around midnight
She anticipated change of direction
Answers were always there

Pamela Haley

Perpetually positive

Outgoing and charismatic

Magnetically adorable

Innocent and naive

Remarkable loyalist

Genuine and true

A tarnished gift

Sentimental and gentle

Tenaciously sweet

A confused single woman

Stella Walker's Acquaintances

Veronica Denson

Forgotten daughter

Exaggerated storyteller

Overshadowed and neglected

Suppressing anger

Seeking self-worth

Fixated to attention

Ignored and undervalued

In and out of dejection

Drowning in the blues

Lost identity

Dwelling in the hardships

Grace Beaumont

World class manipulator
A mind playing tramp
Money hungry and shallow
A body of pleasantries
Carrying a thousand pounds
of pulled and torn guilt

A first prize procrastinator
Fighting temptations
Alluring and magnetic
Horrifying addictions
Unable to love herself
Arrested for indecency

Shame stapled to her
worn out forehead
Pregnant and unstable
Mending all the pieces
Finally surrendering
to a higher almighty power

Stella Walker's Acquaintances

Watching an ocean of tears

Fall to the ground

Someone took her forgiveness

that she could no longer

bear and hold within

Releasing the thousand pounds

to take it day by day

Joshua Bratton

Defined by the dollar

Defined by possessions

Defined by quantity

Defined by numbers

Defined by the notches in the board

Defined by the color of the suit

Defined by the size of the house

Defined by brand names

Defined by his image

Defined by skewed perception

Stella Walker's Acquaintances

Shannon Cole

Lacking confidence
Lacking realness
Stuck in thick glue

Lacking trouble shooting ability
Lacking people skills
Stuck inside her head

Lacking turmoil
Lacking appeal
Stuck in repeat

Lacking a tunnel of depth
Lacking common sense
Stuck finding the missing pieces

Christian Rose

Heart-stopping self-discovery
Bewildering journey
flood of overjoyed tears
Miraculous and marvelous
Walking on a grand path
Appreciative and exhilarating
A thankful perceptive man
Under God's powerful wings
Sitting on precious clouds
Sinking in the scriptures
Spreading the spectacular words

Stella Walker's Acquaintances

Shauna Fields

Full of interpretation
Full of colorful insight
Full of marmalade
Full of mounds of laughter
Full of astonishing sex appeal
Full of a perfect body
Full of an exuberant mind
Full of class and style
Full of intense wit
Full of high standards
Full of herself

BRAEDEN MICHAELS

TREMBLING INSOMNIA

"When fear and anxiety take over your mind, you can't sleep."

Courtney Gray

Cheerful and chirpy
Happy go lucky on the inside
Laid back and treasured
A center made up of syrup
Gracious and thoughtful
The girl two doors down
One boyfriend in high school
Considerate and lovey-dovey
Amicable and good-humored
Boyfriend becomes husband
Mother of three non-stop talking girls
Proud and dazzling creator
Fifty years of a rock steady marriage
Proof of love

Stella Walker's Acquaintances

Devlin Haze

Mistress of manipulation
Teeth like six-inch nails
Scorned and vindictive
A vile bombastic air
Ferocious and cold as ice
19th century gambling thief
A leach in the thick of the night
Deceptive with stained edges
Hungry and thirsty for greed
Invisible spikes in her neck
Voluptuous and poisonous
Hurricanes and monsters dance
in her soul guzzling scotch

Bryant Nash

Sculpted like Goliath

Often glued in his distorted mind

Extraordinary dexterity

Obnoxious obsessive leader

Infatuated with Miss James

No was a word not in his vocabulary

Carried a lava like charm

A monstrous dictating voice

Courting her with a symphony

Comparing her to a dove

A man who does not give up

Wendy Harper

Compared to a caricature
Zealous and abundant
Dedicated sweetheart
A child in the center
Adorable and flirty
Constantly talking
Chirpy and uplifting
But doesn't hear herself
Too much for most
Misunderstood

Stuart Bagley

Completely childish

A sophomoric sense of humor

Constantly wasting time

Goalless wanderer

A sack of potatoes on the couch

Wishing to live in a TV

Work not in vocabulary

Between his 20's and 30's

A bleak future

Relies too much on others

Lives in fantasy land

Scared of reality

Finally looking within

Sonya Applegate

Incredibly calculating
Automatic forethought
Tattooed up and down
Long auburn carefree hair
Intellectually appealing
Layers of sensitivity
Intoxicating voice
Headstrong and domineering
Delicate as ancient glass
Sweet as apple pie

Amber Ponder

Dynamic and stunning

Career oriented and focused

A thick business mind

Extensive vocabulary

Dollar and status driven

Lacking a lover

Extremely intimidating

Intentionally over worked

Constantly occupied

to avoid an ounce of loneliness

Stella Walker's Acquaintances

Katrina Larkin

Additionally, I'm a babbling extrovert

Furthermore, I'm a cunning biologist

Above and beyond, I'm cut-throat

I'm in conjunction with invisible integers

Display manners like a 18th century surgeon

Dissecting emotions like a psychologist

Sitting side by side with top notch analysts

Typically ignoring run on sentences

Extremely clinical in problem solving

Rational to digits, irrational behind doors

Walking with an exorbitant amount of energy

No consumption of lethal stamina drink needed

A well-known documented efficiency expert

Full of propositions and commotion

Slip inside my carnival enterprise like mind

Witchcraft in my sturdy right hand

A strong appetite for methodologies

Craving a cookie cutter and routine lover

Pareto charts in my tight left hand

Lack moxie and enthusiasm at moments

Intellectually driven by the power of knowledge

Scratch that, strive for the application

I'm the sun in the wintertime

Grin for the bewitching scientist

Stella Walker

Whiplashed with sex appeal
A romantic traditionalist
Made from tulips and sugar
A ballroom dancing princess
Draped in a lavender dress
Scorching from head to toe
Pleasant and engaging chats
Up until 3am twirling her hair
A delicate but vibrant smile
An armor inner strength
Bluesy and soft jazz soul
Billie Holiday playing in her
erotic and adorable mind
A woman of excellence
Diverse and stimulating

Stella Walker's Acquaintances

Nia Horne

She drifts into a glitz of speculation

She ran towards a pile of observations

She held onto a mirage of closeness

She lifted her eyelids with the awakened truth

She borrowed sections of a proverb

She ignored the written allegations

She walked down a crusade with bitten nails

She sent the adversary a love letter

She played the diablo torn lyrics

She justified the reasons of the downfall

She fell into darkness with a smug look

Will Scroggs

A crowded mind of fears
Jittery and suspicious
Building up angst and anxiety
Flaring panic button
Phobias in the pockets
Agitations and uneasiness jump
Carrying nightmares like a torch
burning in front of windows
Fright and terror giggle like teens
Trembles forever weighted
Screwed up to the center

Stella Walker's Acquaintances

Michelle Queen

Consistently dense

Ignored by the majority

Full of air and thin skin

A long-term minority

Stuck in illusions

Inability to seek progress

Inattentive and in a fog

Never walks away

Foolish and blind

Lost in a made-up world

Teresa Russell

"All I wanted to do was to have some fun"
A shout to the mind statement
Drinking and pleasure do not mix at 16
Only 10 minutes of so called "love"
I listened to my senseless urges
We broke up after he was born
He said we can't afford "it"
He told me he loved me
Should have listened to my parents
I made the rest of my life difficult
Everything is ten times harder

Stella Walker's Acquaintances

Adrian Sparrow

Swallowed chewed up

and toxic philosophies

Spreading recited

words of love from a pamphlet

All knowing man

A minister of a cult

Obtrusive and vile

A king in his tiny mind

Convicted of extortion

Dying alone in a cell

Knocking at the gates

Falling through a raging cloud

Welcome to ten thousand degrees

Sheri Marshall

Extremely thoughtless

Consistently unappreciative

Strictly self-centered

Completely ungracious

Careless and unmindful

Strong unthankful shell

Faultfinding center

Oblivious to the maximum

One forgetful ingrate

Carrying a file of complaints

SLEEPING WITH ANXIETY

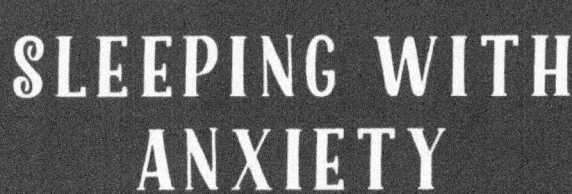

"When you sleep with anxiety, it prevents you from living."

Dana Blough

Born deceiver and storyteller

Creates havoc and consequences

Golden authentic fabricator

Generator of a wide web of deception

Original falsifier and con artist

A leader of noise and turmoil

Shaking cynical bloodhound

Dressed as a loud pretender

A misfit among the thieves

Wearing rebellion as a trench coat

A cold villain underneath

Stella Walker's Acquaintances

Candice Warner

Watching caterpillars smile
Hands digging in the dirt
Ankles in slosh and goo
Filthy and funny tomboy
Tossing dolls away
Playing with plastic trucks
Stacking blocks up high
Mind of an engineer
Embracing complexity
Mastering the Rubik's cube
in under four minutes
Sophisticated and grown
Intimidated by her intellect
Accomplished with accolades
Fearing the all-knowing woman
knowing exactly what she wants

Vanessa Wilkes

Despises the crack of dawn
A vampire in the blood
Grunts sipping on coffee
Alluring on the outside
Angry at the universe
Stuck in contemplation
Dweller of the past
Loves the color black
Confused on the inside
Consistently questioning
her identity and sexuality
Lost like millions

Aralia Desmond

Fragile and quiet
Emotionally abused
Worthless painted
On all four walls
in tragic thick blood
Staring at the letters
Losing herself not
recognizing her
stunning beauty
Tormented and scarred
Rediscovering the
starlight qualities
in her mid-30's
Accepting her dim past
But rebuilt to be stronger
than ever before

Rene Hathaway

Darling of the thrill

Coldness disappears

Sizzling personality

Vivacious and ascending

Tingling excitement

A soaring surge bolts

Incredibly desiring

Sparkling complexion

Provocative to the bone

Risqué and spicy

A tint of crimson

Far away and distant

Crushes my spirit

Kyle Waters

Ambidextrous lover

Walking in a pin stripe suit

Often known as a myth

The prince of style

Scent of grit and New York air

"Did you know your body

spoke to me this morning?"

The doctor of lines

Laid back and cool

Mysterious and smooth as whiskey

Erika Paxton

Slightly obsessed with perfection
Slightly troubled with cleanliness
Slightly infatuated with structure
Slightly engrossed with order
Slightly hooked with simplicity
Slightly hinged with framework
Slightly compelled with arrangements
Slightly fascinated with architecture
Slightly delighted with nature
Slightly charmed with documentaries
Slightly enchanted with socialism
Slightly enamored with practicality
Slightly absorbed with philosophy
Slightly hypnotized with the bare minimum

Stella Walker's Acquaintances

Danny Lancaster

He traded a Jose Canseco
baseball card for a catcher's mitt
He gave his best friend twenty bucks
to ask Robin Metzger out for him
He took his graduation money
to purchase a car that lasted 8 months
He took an ounce of weed
to college to bribe his teacher
He asked his cell mate
for a pack of cigarettes
He got out of prison four years later
and had no clue where he was

Ivory Dennison

Laced in frost
Drawn with a silver tip
Blessed with perfection
Awestruck in alabaster
Bleached with kindness
Dipped with sweetness
Heart shaped like a pearl
A generous soul
Nurturing and polished
Delicate as a china doll
Maybe too fragile
Brittle and frail

Stella Walker's Acquaintances

Josh Musgrave

Mysterious and secretive

Wishing to be with someone else

Fixated on the flowers

in her dark and luxurious hair

Jealous to the center

Slightly obsessed

Suppressing lust

Masking erotic passion

Dancing in his mind

Constantly thinking about her

Kayla Chapman

Inattentive and blind

Only hearing not listening

Not an ounce of adventure

in her skin or veins

Unable to read between the lines

Clueless and ignorant

She became vanilla due to marriage

Making no effort

Using sex as a weapon or a chore

Slowly becoming single

Stella Walker's Acquaintances

Taylor Miles

Sweet and sexy

The way she carries herself

Alluring and radiant

Brick of confidence

Luscious and desirable

Thick backbone

Incredible and divine

Dandelion pupils

Stimulating and arousing

Open minded

Inviting and sensual

Flawless Goddess

Smutty and steamy

Is there more to the surface?

BRAEDEN MICHAELS

Ashton Kerr

Defies brick walls and flaming obstacles
Defies wailing authorities with bullets
Defies plastic and bold labels
Defies political rhetoric with a raised fist
Defies reckless wars without causes
Believes in thinking for yourself

Defies opinions being crammed down throats
Defies yellow charm with painted speeches
Defies religion but embraces holy spirits
Defies tattooed monkeys who nod their heads
Defies thoughts wrapped up in a cardboard box
Believes in thinking for yourself

Defies ignorance and emotional repetition
Defies hatred and destructive patterns
Defies being patronized and twisted sarcasm
Defies written fears and wooden nickels
Defies colored rejection with pointing fingers
Believes in thinking for yourself

Stella Walker's Acquaintances

Emily Castro

Saccharine eyes

Calm in the palms

Quite dashing

Strong demeanor

Highly regarded

Slightly idolized

A stellar prize

Killer looks

Calling me darling

Twinkling intellect

Perception at 18

Dreamed of this man

Settled for three decent qualities

What happened

Starting over

Lynn Hunter

Strong handed feminist

Respected for who she is

Not what she can do or provide

An avid reader

Favorite color green

Collects trinkets

Outspoken and colorful

No nonsense

Thick sensitivity

Lost identity

Constantly inconsistent

Desired and wanted

AWAKENED FAITH

"Faith and hope are always present. They are just buried underneath all the dark."

Laura Peterson

Insanely realistic

Disappearing filter

Unbiased diamond

Bold and daring

Touchy feely

Slightly arrogant

Half inch above confident

Influential and wise

Constantly hiding

Unaware of the potential

Foolish and blind

Rachel Madison

Soothing erotic voice

A tender but a hurricane of a soul

Roaming dark pastures

Absorbing nature

Delicate heartbeats

Alluring soft skin

Falling deep in her magical eyes

Playing within her diamond circus

Captivated by her perceptiveness

Appreciating her ocean tears

One exotic and magnificent woman

Charlene Benton

Royal basket case

A witch with a nerve-racking itch

Overbearing and overrated

Chronic exaggerator

Hot and cold

An emotional extremist

Never easy and warm

Unsolved Rubik's cube

Delirious and frantic

Hates change

A man hater

Forever single

Stella Walker's Acquaintances

Jackson Cash

A rugged southern charm
Potent as whiskey and honey
Personality dipped in marmalade
Attached is his magnetic intellect
A polarizing myth and superhero
Drowns in sensuality and appeal
Casting shadows of perfection
chiseled from head to toe
endearing and rich qualities
A man with a sense of wonder
laced in humility and honesty
Integrity tattooed to his rainbow soul
A warrior from the blazing sun
seeking humanity and kindness
waiting for his other half to melt his heart

Felicia James

Cinderella imitator
Lover of the blush sky
Infatuated with autumn leaves
Favorite color orange
Exhilarating conversationalist
Reads two books a week
Collects stuffed unicorns
Glides to rhythm and blues
A scent of cherry blossom
Excels in performing arts
Craving the center stage

Andrea Carter

Dazzling personality

A perfect ten

Gorgeous from head to toe

A sexy delight

Graceful and precious

A lovely voice

Splendid and superb

A fascinating lady

Elegant and fascinating

A magnificent aura

Delicate and strong

A sensational sight

Carol Holden

Second best

Third place

A small unseen ribbon

Just a contestant

Carrying a chip on her shoulder

Tons of weight

Mediocre and average

Never enough

Depressed and lonely

Trying too hard

Desolate and desperate

In every decade

Tarantula Kid

A legendary high-flyer
Hall of fame luchador
Delivering knife edge chops
Master of the swanton dive
Decorated knee strikes
Thousands applaud
Spinning drop kicks
Flapjack punches
Compared to the Great Muta
Mil Máscaras and Mr. Wrestling
A man of 1,001 moves
World class champion
Respected among his own

BRAEDEN MICHAELS

Ariana Mays

She's the valentine
of the beloved sky
Twirling and flipping
Hanging on to her
lover of lush air
Dangling for hand claps
of a circus crowd
She's the mystical flame
of the enchanted air
Rare and a gem
Entwined in elegance
Strikingly amazing
A treasured Goddess

Stella Walker's Acquaintances

Bradford Stills

I'm bullheaded with spite between my teeth
Occasionally difficult and brittle
I play on the wrong side of danger
I should get a prize for being someone else

Stalking sounds of restlessness
Crude and subdued on the outside
Dabbling with strawberry temptations
I should get a prize for being someone else

Hollow and fragile on the inside
Frequently sleeping with exploitations
I'm regularly running from my demons
I should get a prize for being someone else

Blinking every two seconds frantically
Clutter and disarray seeping
I'm a wreck that no one wants to know
I should get a prize for being someone else

Brooke Fox

Vivacious curves

Buttermilk tan

Alluring lips

Seductive strut

High maintenance

Seeking man of wealth

Image priority number one

Plastic from head to toe

Empty personality

Low self esteem

Dead inside

Marie Lightletter

Absolutely lazy

High expectations

Self-centered

Uses her body as a weapon

A stunning hypocrite

Dangerously promiscuous

Inside her tiny head

She worked once as a hostess

for only two weeks

Demanding to take a break

between 5pm and 7pm

Due to an empty belly

Oblivious to the purpose

for her part time job

BRAEDEN MICHAELS

Thomas Ritter

Brother of Chuck
Son of Adam and Dinah
Dedicated student
Stunning Aquarius
Driven by morals
Structured and by the book
Aspiring Mechanical Engineer
Meticulous and OCD
Order and cleanliness
SAT scores 1475
Dreams at seventeen
Is Michelle the center piece?

Stella Walker's Acquaintances

Carmela Moss

A queen of sarcastic hearts
Withdrawn and cryptic
A gloomy black eye
from insomnia and anxiety
A condescending dancer
wearing stockings of
stretched out distress
Fulfilling voids for others
Defined by her name
with twenty-dollar bills
Treating men as toys
with high expectations
Allowing her center to
turn into granite

Mayfield Barnes

A single righteous man
Intuitive thinker
A sexual night crawler
Inside his head
A cerebral sniper
Pacing among the cells
wearing an orange jumpsuit
A tattoo of a laughing demon
Convicted of manslaughter
Killing his girlfriend
for not cleaning the dishes

Stella Walker's Acquaintances

Bryce Powers

The shaman of seduction
Ayatollah of luscious souls
The prince of pleasure
21st Century Don Juan
Physically focused
Creating an iconic body
Lean and trim
Muscle on muscle
Beautifully molded
60-minute man
The king of midnight

SPARKLING LIGHT

"You will find the light when you discover your identity."

BRAEDEN MICHAELS

Bram Hawthorn

A thunderstruck brawler
Braun and massive
Legs like tree trunks
A monster among men
Face of destruction
Lining up tombstones
for his enemies
A walking nightmare
Ticking like a bomb
A reckless warrior
Clenching fists of anger
Built up with lava and rage
A deranged creature
Misunderstood and confused
Reacting to skewed
and thin perception

Stella Walker's Acquaintances

Chase Carmichael

Larger than life personality

A plush entertainer

Clever and witty to the brim

A craving to be liked by many

Itching to be center of attention

Crossing an incident

A monumental accident

Tear jerking outcome

Reasons unknown suicide

Perfect on the outside

Alone on the inside

Crystal Diamond

From the bottom of a popcorn box
you can hear her high pitch voice
Non-stop talking china doll
Full of a twenty-four-hour energy drink
Delicate as a single pink rose
A lover of the circus and antiques
Captivating scent of a brand-new car
Exuberant and chipper
An admirer of Beatles lyrics and Dylan
Devoted woman to her husband
Mother of two innocent boys

Stella Walker's Acquaintances

Elias Stone

Overplayed copycat
Natural born follower
A stone-cold soldier
Immoral degenerate
Disrespectful to authority
Wearing entitlement
like a gold chain around
his young ignorant neck
Expecting grand gestures
from the overblown world
The gold chain was stolen

Mia Amore

Enigmatic wandering light
A lost breath of fresh air
Profound and intellectual
A divine blacktop soul
Heart carved from clouds
A distant precious road
Fearless and troubled
A roaring laughter
Treasured candle of love
Dedicated and persistent
A wanderlust masterpiece
Blooming fascination
A secret admirer of her core

Stella Walker's Acquaintances

Sylvester Mareno

Animated shadow boxing smile
Swollen death grip eyes
Incarcerated and maniacal
Slippery hands like an octopus
A mind from the Colombo family
Dressed in Joseph Banks suits
Smooth as Jack Daniels
Distinguished hypnotic voice
Born as a rugged thief
Low key and convicted
of breaking innocent hearts

Sabrina Bates

Unforgiving and unforgettable

Poisonous and preposterous

Venomous and vicious

Deadly and daring

Calm and collected

Insensitive and indescribable

Miserable and maniacal

Sick and stubborn

Twisted and tenacious

Whiplashed and withering

Stella Walker's Acquaintances

Haley Richman

Adorably rambunctious

Wildly ear splitting

Blustery primitive

Cheerful and adolescent

Full of enthusiasm

Bright and vivacious

Candy-coated spirit

Amusing and lively

Gut-busting laugh

A tearful joker

Audrey Maxwell

Sweet little darling
Sipping tea from her cup
Deep thoughts on her rocking chair
Nose stuck in a Dickinson book
Style in her fingertips
Turning page after page
Wrapped up in forever
Coddling lukewarm memories
Counting grandchildren and lost ones
Guided by an inward candle
Unforgettable and refreshing

Stella Walker's Acquaintances

Thompson Perry

Emphatically pretentious
Irrationally presumptuous
Consistently audacious
Logically constricted
Evidentially precarious
Clearly problematic
Constantly ambiguous
Borderline hazardous
Extremely indecisive
Ridiculously outlandish
Classically bizarre
Extraordinarily offbeat
Commonly erratic
Vividly unaccountable
Particularly mystifying
Undeniably perplexing
Typically uncanny

Penelope Cross

Sensitive to light
Sensitive to staring eyes
Sensitive to skin on skin
Sensitive to the word love
Sensitive to lost memories
Sensitive to found stars
Sensitive to the word hate
Sensitive to newness
Sensitive to camouflage
Sensitive to crowded agendas

Stella Walker's Acquaintances

Angela Blackledge

Revved up from her education
Admiring the inward bookworm
Dressed up in articulate clothing
Drawn to her stimulating vocabulary
Browsing through endless books
Gazing at her from seconds to minutes
Trying to find the gumption within
Clearing the lump in my throat
Tossing the words in the vault
"Can I check out this book?"

Jazz Brown

Gliding into a smog
Pouring firewater into a shot glass
Exchanging gossip over
mixed drinks wrapped around
a mesmerizing saxophone
Overheating remarks on Socrates
Reciting lines from the book of Proverbs
Observing the couple in the
Deep chocolate booth sipping
On luscious martinis and chain smoke
to the sound of the rhapsody
Entwined notes and soulful galore
Hypnotized to his shuffling feet
as he sways back and forth
nicknaming him Jazz Brown
An entertainer in the center of the heart
Playing for thousands over decades
Married to his sweet saxophone

Stella Walker's Acquaintances

April Winter

She is exhausted from spilling ink
She is uncertain with her fingertips
She is wobbly and shaking on the inside
She is powerless from the past
She is flimsy as a thin piece of paper
Sing me a song for wide hope
Sing me a song for stretched out faith

She is frail within her bones
She is isolated from the rattle
She is licking her wounds quietly
She is aching for companionship
She is comfortless and abandoned
Sing me a song of freedom
Sing me a song without chains

She is tangled up in desolation
She is withdrawn and torn down
She is a tragedy without a witness
She is reclusive and friendless
She is a sky without clouds
Sing me a song for change
Sing me a song for healing

BRAEDEN MICHAELS

Tyson Walcott

Feverishly neurotic
Scientific and algebraic
Consistently nervous
Slightly uptight and cautious
Exponentially gifted
A master of digitalization
Color coded memory
Dependable and rational
Exceptional logic
Requires exactness and clarity
Black and white, no gray
Culturally particular
Quite capable and accomplished
Polished and distinctive
Viewed as thoroughly sterile
A civilized and knowledgeable man

Stella Walker's Acquaintances

Beth Patrick

I'm reminded of my splotchy blunders
I confess I speak with a fatigued tongue
I'm forewarned of my personal thorns
I acknowledge that I fear closeness
I'm notified of my discolored short comings
I confided with my disappearing aurora
I'm advised of my lack of listening skills
I shed weary and catatonic skin
I'm made aware of my little success
I spill ink of my sufferings and losses

BRAEDEN MICHAELS

Fiona Marks

I'm a 4am sleepwalker with a love for mint chocolate chip ice cream
I'm a skydiver in the fall and hibernate in the white of winter
I play the acoustic guitar and hum the words of the broken hearted
I read poems of Rosetti in my rocking chair and nibble on homemade apple pie
I'm a soft-spoken liberal with philosophies dancing in my mind
I'm a freelance photographer and dabble in graphic arts
I'm a lover of board games and solitaire
I'm a mother of a child that has never met her abusive father
I have scars and bruises to prove it

Stella Walker's Acquaintances

Harper Mullins

I'm habitually shy and cautious
I'm serene and stuck in sentences
Excuse me, I'm in awe of you

I'm carefully hesitant and quiet
I'm placid and cemented in paragraphs
Excuse me, I admire you

I'm thoroughly fearful and discrete
I'm tentative and fastened in paraphrases
Excuse me, I adore you

I'm rationally reserved and hushed
I'm hesitant and jumbled in emotions
Excuse me, I cherish you

I'm gingerly modest and demure
I'm indecisive and scrambled in sentiments
Excuse me, I'm in love with you

EPILOGUE

Through the trials and tribulations, Stella's scars were no longer jagged. A degree hung on her wall. She could count her milestones and accomplishments on both hands. She walked around with a glow. Stella refused to allow becoming a widow to define her. The word "widow" was no longer engraved on her arm. There were more appropriate words attached to her essence such as "warrior" and "conqueror". She was no longer drowning in her sorrow. Stella was born to swim against the current in any storm.

On the wall above her bed, a poem in a frame continues to light up her room.

Stella Walker's Acquaintances

Captivating freckles
A grand and vibrant smile
Her acquaintances loved her glow
Motivated by her young children
A strong admiration of history
Mistress of music and harmony
Loves hard and grips tight
Playing with the fireflies
Staring at her beauty from a far
Men steer clear from the intensity
Not comprehending her purpose
Unable to grasp her identity
Naturally, they become "acquaintances"
To the fear of embracing love
Death has made sensitivity thick
No one will ever see how Stella loves
with her everlasting spirit.

www.ingramcontent.com/pod-product-compliance
Lightning Source LLC
Chambersburg PA
CBHW032018040426
42448CB00006B/659